BERNARD LYONS
ASTROLOGY

Navigating the Cosmic Blueprint
(2024 Guide for Beginners)

Copyright © 2024 by Bernard Lyons

All rights reserved. No part of this publication may be reproduced, stored or transmitted in any form or by any means, electronic, mechanical, photocopying, recording, scanning, or otherwise without written permission from the publisher. It is illegal to copy this book, post it to a website, or distribute it by any other means without permission.

Bernard Lyons asserts the moral right to be identified as the author of this work.

First edition

This book was professionally typeset on Reedsy. Find out more at reedsy.com

Contents

1 Degrees, Aspects and Orbs	1
Identifying the degree in your chart	1
Planetary aspects (aka planetary angles)	3
Conjunctions, sextiles, squares, trines and oppositions	4
The condition of a planet	8
Interpreting the aspects	9
Summary	12
2 Aspect and the Chart Pattern	13
Major Aspects Pattern	13
The T-Square	14
Grand Trine	15
The Yod	17
The Mystic Rectangle	19
The Kite	22
Major Chart Patterns	23
See-Saw Configuration:	24
Tripod/Splay Configuration:	24
Locomotive Pattern:	24
Bucket Configuration:	24
Bundle/Wedge Setup:	25
Splash Configuration:	25
3 Retrograde Planets	27
What cause a retrograde?	27
How do planet retrograde affect us?	28

The meaning of retrograde	29
Mercury in Retrograde	30
Venus in Retrograde	30
Mars in Retrograde	31
Jupiter in Retrograde	32
Uranus in Retrograde	33
Neptune in Retrograde	34
Pluto in Retrograde	34
The Three Iterations of a Retrograde	36
4 The Moon's Nodes	40
Engaging with the Moon's Nodes	41
Decoding the Significance of the Moon's Nodes	42

1

Degrees, Aspects and Orbs

Identifying the degree in your chart

Determining the degrees in your astrological chart is essential for a comprehensive understanding of Western astrology. In Western astrology, horoscope charts are circular, encompassing 360 degrees and divided into 12 equal segments representing signs and houses. Each of these sections consists of 30 degrees, and astrologers use a range of 0 to 29 degrees, not 1 to 30. Furthermore, each degree is further divided into minutes and seconds, spanning from 00.00 to 29.59 within a sign, always counted anticlockwise.

For instance, if we consider the notation 14° 23′ 33″, it indicates the Sun positioned at 14 degrees, 23 minutes, and 33 seconds in the sign of Aries. Every degree in the 360-degree circle potentially corresponds to a planet, cusp, or other significant point.

Returning to your birth chart, it's crucial to record the degrees at which each planet resides. Utilize the provided table to fill in the following information (excluding seconds):

- My Sun is at _____ degrees and _____ minutes of _____ (sign)
- My Moon is at _____ degrees and _____ minutes of _____ (sign)
- My ascendant is at _____ degrees and _____ minutes of _____ (sign)
- My Mercury is at _____ degrees and _____ minutes of _____ (sign)
- My Venus is at _____ degrees and _____ minutes of _____ (sign)
- My Mars is at _____ degrees and _____ minutes of _____ (sign)
- My Jupiter is at _____ degrees and _____ minutes of _____ (sign)
- My Saturn is at _____ degrees and _____ minutes of _____ (sign)
- My Uranus is at _____ degrees and _____ minutes of _____ (sign)
- My Neptune is at _____ degrees and _____ minutes of _____ (sign)
- My Pluto is at _____ degrees and _____ minutes of _____ (sign)

Calculating these degrees serves multiple purposes:

1. **Aspect Calculation:** It helps calculate the angles, known as aspects, between planets in your chart, indicating how they connect or form conjunctions.
2. **Transit Analysis:** It enables the measurement of angles

(aspects) that transiting planets (current sky positions) form with your chart or another individual's chart.
3. **Compatibility Examination:** Understanding how someone else's planets aspect yours is crucial for compatibility analysis.
4. **Current Sky Analysis:** By measuring how transiting planets aspect each other, you gain insights into the current celestial dynamics.

These angles or aspects play a pivotal role in interpreting the intricate relationships and influences within your astrological chart.

Planetary aspects (aka planetary angles)

Celestial connections, commonly known as planetary aspects or angles, denote the relationships between two planets within an astrological chart. These connections are determined by examining the degrees occupied by each planet. For instance, if a planet resides at 15 degrees in a Fire or Air sign and another planet is positioned approximately at 15 degrees (within a 5-degree range on either side) of a Fire or Air sign, they are considered to be in a favorable and harmonious aspect. This alignment holds true for Fire and Fire, Air and Air, as well as Fire and Air combinations.

Similarly, if planets are within 5 degrees of each other in Earth or Water signs, they are also deemed to be in an easy and harmonious aspect. Conversely, if one or more planets are situated at, for example, 23 degrees in a Water sign, and there is another planet or more at around 23 degrees (within a 5-degree range) of a Fire or Air sign, these planets are considered to be in a challenging aspect to each other.

The interpretation of aspects holds significant importance in understanding an astrological chart. These connections reveal the dynamics of planetary and sign energies. By analyzing the aspects formed between two planets or between planets and the four chart angles, one can discern whether challenges or harmonious flow will characterize specific life aspects. Without a grasp of degrees and aspects, a comprehensive understanding of one's own chart or that of others remains elusive.

Conjunctions, sextiles, squares, trines and oppositions

In fundamental astrology, five primary aspects are employed: conjunctions, sextiles, squares, trines, and oppositions. However, it's important to note that the term "aspect" essentially means 'view.' While technically, a conjunction may not be classified as an aspect since two adjacent planets cannot have a direct line of sight to each other, the term "conjunctions and aspects" is commonly used, treating conjunctions as an aspect.

When examining the central circle of your astrological chart, you'll observe lines connecting the planets, each adorned with glyphs representing the various aspects. Similar to signs and planets, these aspects are symbolized in the chart. The provided table illustrates the glyphs for each aspect and the degree separation required for planets and points to form these connections.

Aspect name | Glyph | Degrees apart

Conjunction | 0 degrees
   Sextile | 60 degrees
   Square | 90 degrees
   Trine | 120 degrees
   Opposition | 180 degrees

Upon scrutinizing your chart, you may identify all five aspects or only a selection. Calculating aspects involves assessing the degrees at which planets are positioned. A conjunction occurs when a planet is located next to another (within 5 degrees), a sextile when it's around the same degree two signs away, a square when it's around the same degree three signs away, a trine when it's around the same degree four signs away, and an opposition when it's directly opposite.

Verification of aspects on your chart can also be done by checking the degree count. Examine the grid beneath your birth chart to swiftly determine the aspects your planets form with others. The subsequent section provides a description of each of the five aspects along with their corresponding glyphs. Additionally, before delving further, it's essential to understand the term "orb," which refers to the 'range of degrees.'

Conjunction:

In astrology, a conjunction occurs when two or more planets align precisely at the same degree, with an 8-degree allowance (10 degrees if the Sun and/or Moon are part of the alignment). For instance, if one planet is at 22 degrees of Leo and another at 26 degrees of Leo, they are considered conjunct. It's worth noting that planets can also form conjunctions in different zodiac signs. The ease or challenge of a conjunction depends on the specific planets involved. For example, a Sun-Venus conjunction is likely to be effortless, while a Venus-Saturn conjunction may pose more challenges. However, interpretations should remain open-minded as outcomes can vary.

Sextile:

A sextile is an aspect where planets are positioned 60 degrees apart in either direction, essentially two signs apart and sharing the same degree (with a 5-degree allowance, or 6 if the Sun and/or Moon are part of the configuration). Sextiles are considered easy aspects, fostering a productive and dynamic flow of energy between the involved planets.

Square:

The square aspect occurs when planets are 90 degrees apart in either direction, equivalent to being three signs apart and sharing the same degree, with a 5-degree allowance (or 10 if the Sun and/or Moon are in the mix). Squares are challenging aspects, signifying a clash between the planets involved. Despite the challenges, squares can instigate irritation that leads to transformative change.

Trine:

In astrology, a trine is present when planets are 120 degrees apart in either direction, meaning they are four signs apart and share the same degree, with a 5-degree allowance (or 10 if the Sun and/or Moon are part of the alignment). Trines are considered easy and flowing aspects, indicating harmonious interactions between the planets. However, they can also foster complacency if not approached with awareness.

Opposition:

In astrology, an opposition occurs when planets are positioned 180 degrees apart, essentially located on opposite sides of the chart at the same degree, with a 5-degree allowance (or 10 if the Sun and/or Moon are part of the alignment). Typically viewed as challenging aspects, it's crucial to recognize that oppositional planets always fall within compatible elemental categories. Fire signs oppose Air signs, and Earth signs oppose Water signs. This can result in both clashes and harmonious dynamics, as opposites have the potential to attract. Furthermore, oppositions bring forth both sides of the issues indicated by the involved planets, offering a comprehensive perspective that can be beneficial.

To test your understanding of degrees and aspects, consider the following question (keeping in mind that there are 30 degrees in a sign and 12 signs):

Question: If your Sun is at 12 Gemini and your Venus is at 12 Leo (two signs later), how many degrees apart are they?

Hint: Proceed through the signs in the traditional order of Aries, Taurus, Gemini, Cancer, Leo, Virgo, Libra, Scorpio, Sagittarius, Capricorn, Aquarius, and Pisces to find your answer.

Answer: Your Sun and Venus would be 60 degrees apart, constituting a sextile aspect.

The condition of a planet

The state or "condition" of a planet is a topic frequently discussed by astrologers, referring to the kind of situation or state it finds itself in. Traditionally, this assessment would involve considering its dignity, as indicated by the dignity table. However, in a more casual sense, a significant factor influencing a planet's condition is the nature of the aspects it forms with other planets. The key question is whether it's in harmony, indicated by sextiles and trines, or facing challenges, marked by squares and oppositions.

As discussed earlier, trines and sextiles are harmonious aspects, implying an effortless flow between planets and a state of harmony rather than conflict. When examining your chart, the compatibility of elements, such as Fire/Air and Earth/Water, becomes apparent through the 60 degrees of a sextile (two signs) and 120 degrees of a trine (four signs). Planets in compatible elements make sextiles and trines, while those in incompatible elements form squares.

The square aspect is considered the most challenging, evoking discomfort or tension that can be felt deeply. Planets in square aspects present issues that act as focal points for learning and growth. Squares force individuals to confront and address problems, serving as catalysts for personal evolution.

Conjunctions and oppositions, as mentioned earlier, can have varied effects depending on the specific planets involved. It's crucial to recognize that aspects can be observed in different ways, including those formed between planets in one's own chart, between the transiting planets and the planets in one's chart, and even among the transiting planets themselves. Understanding these aspects provides insights into the energetic dynamics at play, both personally and globally. Further details on transiting aspects will be explored in Chapter 7.

Interpreting the aspects

Deciphering the aspects involves considering the inherent ease or difficulty associated with each planet, influencing our interpretation of these connections. For instance, a Moon (feelings) square Venus (love) imparts a lighter energy compared to, let's say, Venus (love) square Saturn (heavy-duty karma), where the involvement of Mars, Saturn, or outer planets intensifies the energy.

An alternative approach is to substitute 'sextile' or 'trine' with 'is in harmony with' and 'square' or 'opposition' with 'is clashing with.' For example, Venus square Pluto becomes Venus is clashing with Pluto, while Mercury trine Jupiter becomes Mercury is in harmony with Jupiter.

To interpret Venus square Pluto in a birth chart, consider the following:

1. What does Venus represent? (Love, money, lessons?)
2. In which zodiac sign is Venus placed? (Understanding the sign's meaning adds depth.)
3. In which astrological house is Venus located? (The house's meaning contributes another layer of information.)
4. What does Pluto signify? (Power, transformation, obsession?)
5. In which zodiac sign is Pluto positioned?
6. In which astrological house is Pluto situated?

On a birth chart, a planet's full potential might be hindered if squared by Mars (anger), Saturn (depression), Uranus (chaos), Neptune (confusion), or Pluto (intense transformation). For instance, someone with Venus in Gemini, known for chattiness and positivity, may not exhibit the typical Gemini traits if Venus is squared by stern Saturn, whereas a Venus trined by Jupiter might display the full charm of Gemini.

Consider this example: someone with Venus harmoniously connected (sextile or trine) to Jupiter, a joyful planet, will manifest a distinct Venus compared to someone with Venus clashing (squaring or opposing) with intense Pluto.

It's essential to grasp the subtlety that no planet is inherently good or bad. When planets clash, the negative traits may surface, while harmonious aspects allow the best qualities to shine. Remember, sextiles and trines denote flowing energies, while squares and oppositions indicate clashes.

With 90 possible basic aspects, interpretations have filled entire books. For further exploration, Sue Tompkin's "Aspects In Astrology" is recommended to deepen your understanding beyond this book's scope.

Unaspected Planets

Planets may exist without forming connections to others within an acceptable range, meaning they don't create any aspects with fellow planets. In such instances, they are labeled as "unaspected," implying that they operate independently, free from the influence of other celestial bodies. Unaspected planets follow their own narrative, marching to a distinct rhythm and pursuing their unique trajectory.

It's worth noting that individuals with an unaspected Sun, in particular, tend to embody a distinctive quality, often considered mavericks who defy societal norms and constraints. This doesn't necessarily categorize them as eccentric; rather, it significantly amplifies their distinctiveness. These are the individuals who tend to think beyond conventional boundaries.

For those still grappling with the understanding of degrees and aspects, a visual explanation is available in a video on theastrologybook.com/degreesaspects.

Summary

Congratulations! You are now officially embarking on the journey to becoming a proficient astrologer. While mastering the signs and planets is fundamental, delving into the intricacies of degrees and aspects serves as the crowning achievement in the realm of astrology.

When initially examining aspects on your chart or that of others, consider the following:
  - Conjunctions can be either smooth or challenging, contingent on the specific planets involved. For instance, Saturn conjoining with the Sun might pose more difficulty than, let's say, Jupiter aligning with the Sun.
  - Trines and sextiles offer ease, blending energies harmoniously. Pairing pleasing planets like Venus and Jupiter in a trine, for example, doubles the potential for joy.
  - Even seemingly challenging trines, such as Venus trine Saturn or Saturn trine Pluto, bring positive influences despite the individual challenges posed by Saturn and Pluto.
  - Squares and oppositions introduce more complexities. For instance, the Sun square Mars can bring forth the less favorable aspects of both planets, such as the Sun's egotism and Mars's aggression.

2

Aspect and the Chart Pattern

Now, let's briefly explore various configurations and arrangements that emerge from the positions of planets in a birth chart, offering further insights into how these celestial bodies influence your astrological landscape. When three or more planets establish connections through aspects, they create distinct patterns, unraveling additional layers of information beyond the basic aspects you've already familiarized yourself with. For instance, recognizing that a square denotes a challenge is foundational, but encountering a T-square aspect pattern introduces an even more intricate set of challenges.

Major Aspects Pattern

Several major aspect patterns, such as the Grand Trine, T-Square, Yod, and Kite, contribute to the intricate tapestry of a birth chart, warranting a closer examination.

The T-Square

Let's delve into the T-Square, a pattern characterized by two planets positioned in opposition, with a third planet situated 'in the middle' of these opposing planets, forming squares with both. Refer to the illustration on the subsequent page for clarity. While a single square presents challenges, the T-Square intensifies the complexity by featuring not one, but two squares and an opposition. This arrangement instigates a dynamic interplay of conflicting forces within the T-Square.

Returning to your birth chart, if a T-Square is present, it's essential to scrutinize all the elements involved—the planets, zodiac signs, and houses. This comprehensive analysis aids in constructing a detailed picture of the potential issues that may arise for you.

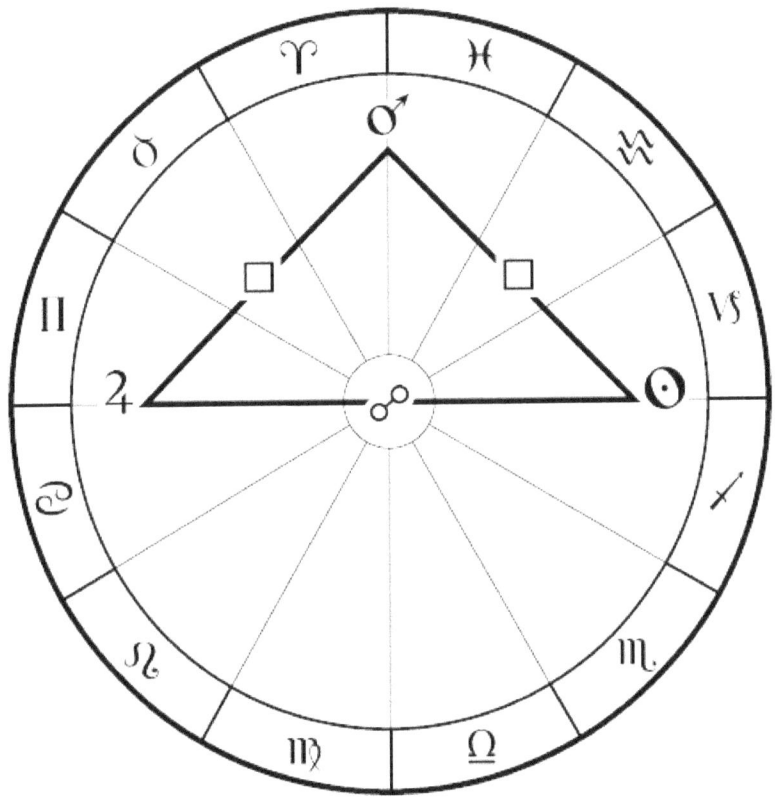

The T-Square Chart

Grand Trine

The Grand Trine is characterized by the connection of three planets through three trines, forming a triangular configuration within the birth chart.

The Grand Trine represents a harmonious flow of energies between the involved planets, akin to individuals holding hands and transmitting love in a circular motion. Planetary influences within a Grand Trine circulate effortlessly, sometimes even excessively.

There are four distinct types of Grand Trine, each corresponding to one of the four elements:
- Fire Grand Trine: Indicates enthusiasm driving productivity and success.
- Earth Grand Trine: Suggests smooth progress through practical and grounded approaches.
- Air Grand Trine: Facilitates the flow of ideas and intellectual pursuits.
- Water Grand Trine: Reflects emotional fluidity and compassion among individuals.

Upon reviewing your birth chart, if you identify a Grand Trine, it may signify a tendency towards laziness, although overall, it's considered a favorable aspect, often seen as a blessing.

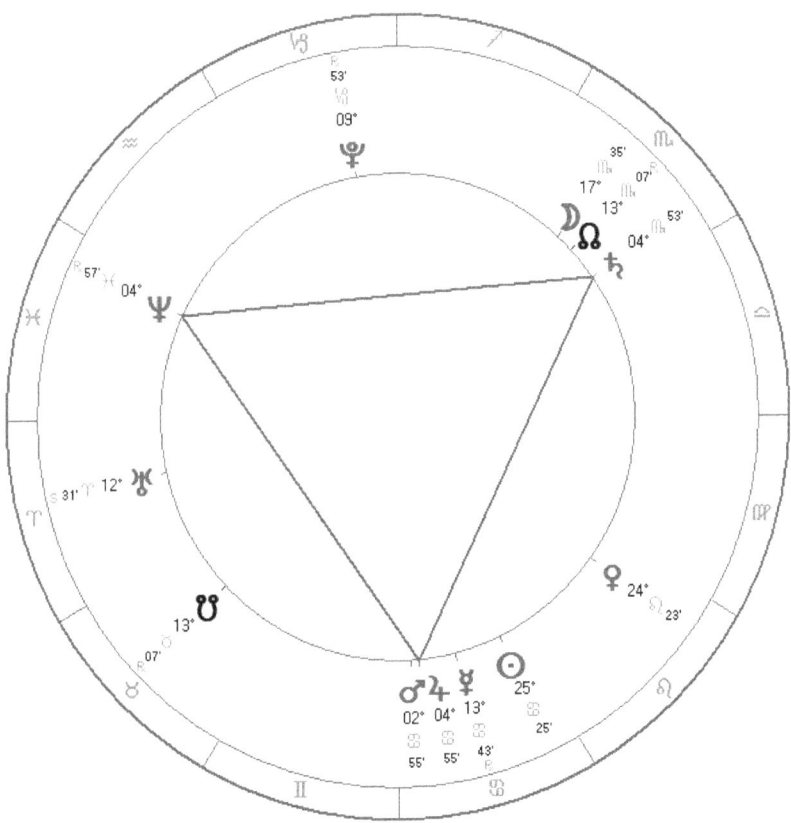

The Grand Trine Chart

The Yod

The Yod is an uncommon aspect involving three planets or other celestial points arranged in a triangular pattern. In this configuration, two planets are in a sextile relationship, while the third forms a quincunx angle (150 degrees apart) with the midpoint of the sextile.

Illustrated in Figure , the Yod is often referred to as the Finger of God, with some interpreting it as an indication of a unique life mission or destiny. However, there are differing opinions on the informativeness of the Yod. While some argue it holds significance, suggesting a distinct purpose, others contend that every individual arrives on Earth with a special mission or destiny, rendering the Yod unnecessary for that realization.

Upon examining your birth chart, check for the presence of a Yod. In its optimal manifestation, a Yod might challenge you to transition from the ease of a sextile to the more challenging dynamics of a quincunx, prompting you to fulfill your distinctive life mission.

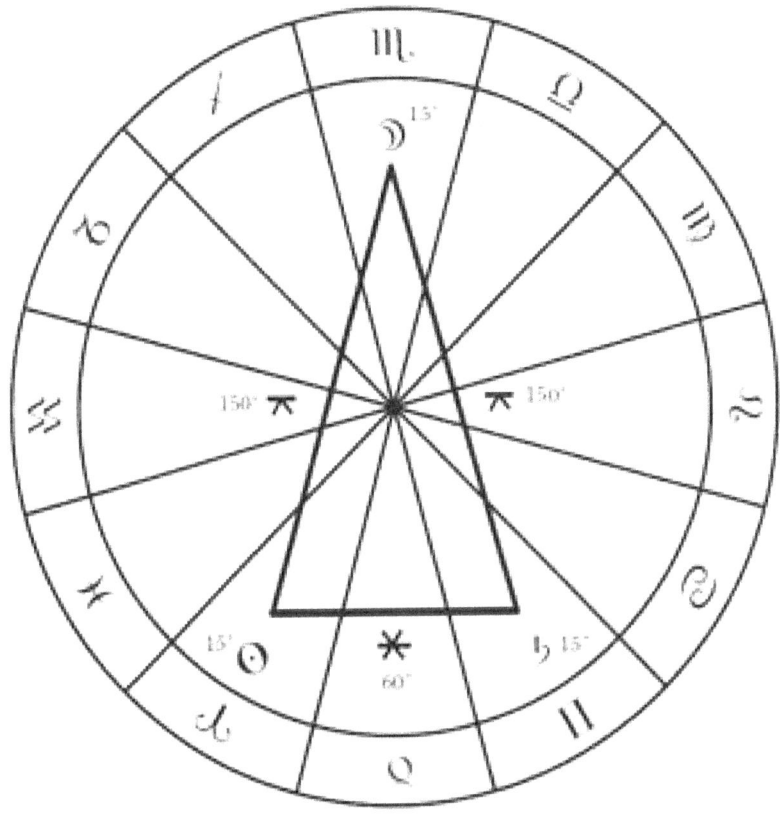

The Yod Chart

The Mystic Rectangle

The Mystic Rectangle is an intriguing pattern that materializes when four or more planets establish connections through sextiles, trines, and oppositions, forming a harmonious geometric arrangement.

As depicted in Figure, the Mystic Rectangle bestows individuals with the capability to excel in various aspects of life, both on a personal and professional level, fostering a continuous flow of energy.

Upon scrutinizing your birth chart, ascertain whether a Mystic Rectangle is present. This particular pattern is reputed to enhance psychic abilities while instilling a profound sense of equilibrium and harmony among the four involved planets.

ASPECT AND THE CHART PATTERN

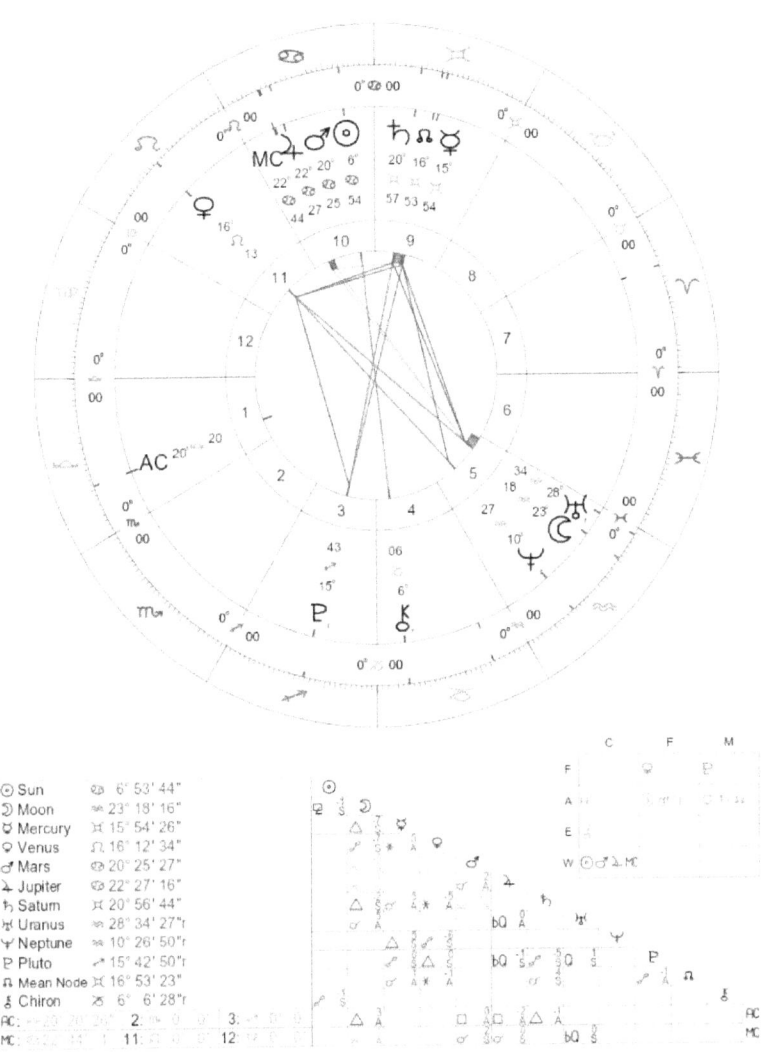

Print chart

The Mystic Rectangle

The Kite

The Kite configuration is essentially a Grand Trine infused with added complexity, featuring a fourth planet that opposes one of the three planets in the Grand Trine while forming sextiles with the other two.

Refer to Figure for a visual representation of the Kite. In this pattern, the Opposition serves a crucial role, acting akin to the grit in an oyster that gives rise to a pearl. While a standalone Grand Trine might offer pleasant energies, it may not necessarily lead to substantial and noteworthy developments. The presence of the Opposition within the Kite imparts a sense of direction and focus to the individual, serving as an anchor for the positive attributes associated with the Grand Trine.

Upon reviewing your birth chart, explore the possibility of a Kite formation. This pattern introduces tension into your chart dynamics, providing an opportunity to leverage and maximize the positive energies it encompasses.

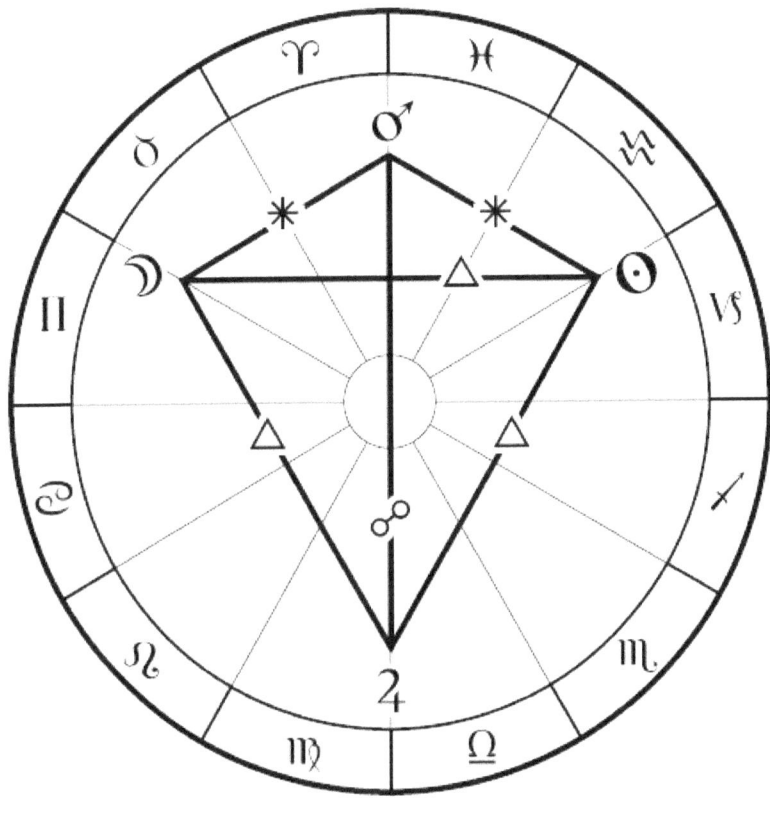

The Kite

Major Chart Patterns

After thoroughly examining your chart, you might observe a concentration of planets in specific areas or significant empty spaces. The subsequent overview offers a concise guide on interpreting different patterns that may emerge.

See-Saw Configuration:

When the planets are distributed across the chart in two opposing groups, it implies the presence of numerous 'opposites' within the individual, potentially manifesting as contradictions. This pattern often signifies a fluctuation or see-sawing between different modes of being.

Tripod/Splay Configuration:

In this arrangement, planets form tight groups of three or four, drawing attention to specific houses within the chart. These highlighted houses may emerge as the most significant or pivotal areas of interest in the individual's life.

Locomotive Pattern:

In the locomotive pattern, all planets cluster together, occupying two-thirds of the chart, leaving the remaining one third, or 120 degrees, vacant. This setup indicates a notable emphasis on one section of the chart, with the unoccupied part receiving less focus.

Bucket Configuration:

The bucket formation occurs when all planets in the chart concentrate on one side, except for a singular planet on the opposite side. The singleton assumes significant importance in the individual's chart, influencing both its expression in the birth chart and the effects during transits by other planets.

Bundle/Wedge Setup:

In this configuration, planets gather within 120 degrees of each other, signifying areas of particular significance. If a considerable number of planets populate a specific section of the chart, the individual's focus in this lifetime will likely center on those areas, taking into account the sign and house in which the bundle or wedge is located.

Splash Configuration:

The splash pattern manifests when planets are evenly distributed across the zodiac or chart. Individuals with this arrangement possess a diverse array of talents and abilities. However, to accomplish their goals effectively, they need to concentrate on one task at a time.

Refer to Figure for a visual representation of the splash pattern. By now, you should have a grasp of the key chart patterns essential for examining your own or someone else's astrological chart.

As you delve into chart analysis more frequently, these patterns may quickly catch your attention. They serve as a visual shorthand, providing valuable insights into the overall character of the chart. Our next exploration will delve into a topic familiar even to non-astrologers – retrograde planets. If you've ever been curious about Mercury retrograde or the significance of retrograde motion in other planets, continue reading!

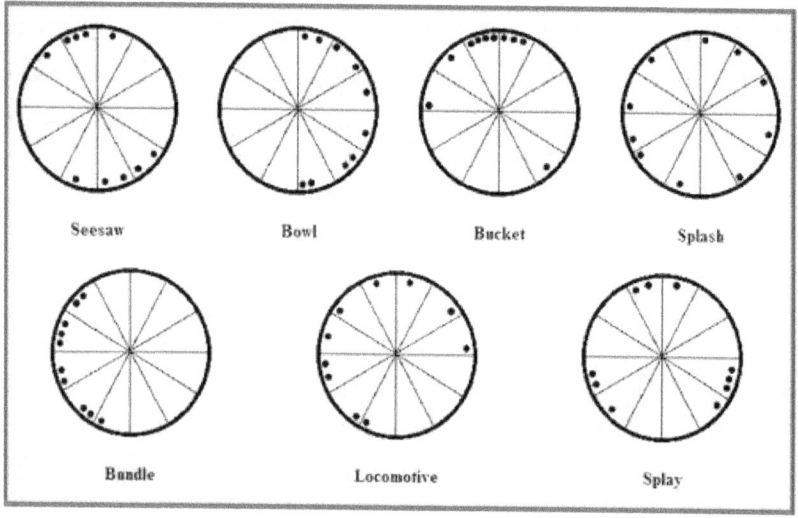

The Major Patterns

3

Retrograde Planets

Now we delve into a facet of astrology that you may already be familiar with. All the celestial bodies, excluding the Sun and the Moon, which are rightly considered luminaries rather than planets, undergo a phenomenon known as 'retrograde' periodically. Retrograde is the apparent backward motion a planet seems to take in the sky, although, in reality, none of the planets move backward in their orbit around the Sun.

What cause a retrograde?

The cause of this retrograde motion can be elucidated quite simply. Picture yourself on a train, and outside your window, a woman is riding a horse a little distance ahead. She is moving swiftly, but the train is moving even faster. As the train advances, you gradually catch up with the woman on the horse. Eventually, you are side by side with her. As the train passes them, the woman and the horse seem to move backward from your perspective.

This analogy illustrates how retrogrades appear from our vantage point. For instance, from Earth, we perceive Mercury ahead, but as Earth moves faster, we catch up and surpass Mercury. During this overtaking process, Mercury seems to reverse its course.

One can anticipate the onset of a retrograde for Venus or Mercury by observing them moving significantly ahead of the Sun in the ephemeris or the night sky. Mercury enters retrograde when it is approximately 14 degrees ahead of the Sun, while Venus turns retrograde when it's about 30 degrees ahead of the Sun. Consequently, instead of progressing forward through the zodiac signs, Mercury seems to backtrack through the sign it was in when the retrograde commenced. Though an illusion, it holds symbolic significance.

How do planet retrograde affect us?

When a planet undergoes retrogradation, there is a pause in its usual progression. You can determine when planets go retrograde by consulting an ephemeris or checking astrological websites, where retrograde planets are designated by a glyph resembling Rx. This period contrasts with our usual relentless forward momentum in the modern world, offering an opportunity to take a breather. During retrograde, energies turn inward.

If a planet is retrograde in your birth chart, you will experience its energy on a deeper, more internal level. Generally, a retrograde planet in your chart indicates energies turned inward, possibly inverted or more introspective. Retrograde planets may exhibit shyness and awkwardness but also possess profound depth and heightened sensitivity.

If you were born during a retrograde, that planet will be retrograde on your birth chart, marked by the symbol . It's natural to question whether retrogrades bring bad luck, but they are neither inherently good nor bad – everything, including planetary backward motion, happens for a reason.

The meaning of retrograde

As you are aware, each planet follows a distinct cycle while orbiting the Sun, accompanied by its own frequency and duration of retrograde motion. The impact of retrogrades on an individual varies based on their birth chart. However, the following descriptions outline the primary themes associated with all planets in retrograde (abbreviated as rx).

To identify any retrograde planets in your chart, examine the list of planets and degrees located at the top right of your birth chart. Retrograde planets are denoted by a red – an R with its tail crossed. In the medical context, this symbol signifies 'prescription,' originating from the Latin word recipere in its imperative form, meaning 'to take back.' It symbolizes the retracement or reclaiming of the involved planet.

Mercury in Retrograde

Mercury retrograde is likely the most well-known of all retrogrades, a phenomenon occurring up to four times annually. As the planet associated with communication, Mercury's reversal can lead to disruptions in communication. However, Mercury retrograde encompasses more than just communication challenges. It serves as an opportunity for reflection, revisiting, editing, and revision – aspects we all need to address periodically.

Rather than wishing away Mercury retrogrades, it is beneficial to examine where they occur in your chart, considering the specific house and planets involved. Consciously engage with these energies by identifying the sign and house of the retrograde and contemplating how that aspect of your life could benefit from a reassessment.

If Mercury retrograde is present in your chart, you may exhibit a thoughtful approach to actions, leaning towards introspection. Writing skills may be a strength, but issues related to writing or self-doubt could also emerge. A distinctive and slightly unconventional sense of humor and communication style is common among individuals with Mercury retrograde.

Venus in Retrograde

Venus retrograde happens approximately once every 18 months and is linked to matters of love. Relationships may experience a strain during Venus retrograde, prompting partners to contemplate the significance of their connection. This period can lead to a newfound appreciation for one another.

Venus, representing values, encourages reevaluation during its retrograde phase. Caution is advised against making significant purchases during Venus retrograde, as changing perspectives on the value of acquired items often ensue.

In a chart, Venus retrograde can be advantageous, fostering the ease of abundance creation. It frequently signifies artistic inclinations or a career in the arts. In a woman's chart, it may symbolize pioneering feminine expression but can also indicate shyness and insecurity.

Mars in Retrograde

Occurs approximately once every two years, Mars retrograde can be challenging as Mars is the planet associated with swift forward movement. The contradiction arises when Mars seems to move backward, contrary to its inherent programming of relentless progression. During Mars retrograde, the sensation of struggling to make progress may be akin to wading through treacle. However, it's worth considering the notion that there might be a purpose in the universe's seemingly chaotic design.

When Mars is retrograde, and you find yourself grappling with tasks, it could be an opportunity to explore the benefits of slowing down. Mars retrograde is particularly relevant as Mars is also linked to anger. On one hand, it presents an occasion to observe how life unfolds when anger is less prevalent. On the other hand, there's a risk of individuals bottling up their anger, which is generally unhealthy.

If Mars retrograde is present in your chart, you might be averse to conflict, less adept at asserting yourself, and inclined towards adopting a peacemaker role. Balancing the avoidance of arguments with expressing suppressed anger constructively is essential.

Jupiter in Retrograde

Renowned astrologer Robert Hand once asserted that there is no such thing as a negative Jupiter transit, and the same sentiment applies to Jupiter retrograde. Despite Jupiter being the planet associated with good luck, interpreting its retrograde phase as a reduction in luck may be misleading. Instead, Jupiter retrograde can be seen as an opportunity to attract more positive fortune into our lives.

For instance, if Jupiter is retrograde in your 3rd house, you may find yourself less talkative than usual. The extended duration of positive thinking that Jupiter offers becomes a focal point during its retrograde phase. Jupiter's more contemplative side emerges, emphasizing inner awareness and spiritual growth over exuberant joy. Jupiter is retrograde for about six months each year.

Individuals with Jupiter retrograde in their chart may hold unconventional life philosophies, and although they believe in and may experience luck, they are less reliant on it. Retrograde Jupiter can lead to a more rebellious approach, while direct Jupiter (non-retrograde) tends to adhere more to conventional rules.

Uranus in Retrograde

Consider this scenario: the planet synonymous with chaos and unpredictability is making its presence felt in your astrological chart, introducing disorder and unexpected twists. When Uranus goes into retrograde, the usual forward momentum of this chaos takes a temporary pause. This doesn't mean it comes to a complete halt; rather, it ceases its trailblazing path through your chart, disrupting planets and traversing houses. Although Uranus is generally a slow-moving planet, during its retrograde phase, it does halt its forward movement, revisiting and perhaps reenacting some of the chaos it caused earlier. The concept of three-pass retrogrades adds depth to these experiences. Uranus experiences retrograde for approximately half the year.

If Uranus retrograde is present in your chart, you might find discomfort in embracing change, even if there's a rebellious inclination within you. There's a tendency to hold back despite the desire for a more defiant approach.

Neptune in Retrograde

Describing Neptune proves challenging due to its elusive nature as the planet associated with mysticism and deception. It's important to note that Neptune undergoes retrograde for about five months annually. Neptune revolves around dreams and visions, and during its backward motion, its sensitivity intensifies.

Neptune is also linked to confusion, especially when it influences one of your planets through aspects like squaring, opposing, or conjoining. Such configurations extend the duration of confusion. Neptune retrograde has the power to unveil truths we may have been reluctant to acknowledge, stripping away any illusions we've created for ourselves. It's a revelation that we've been viewing things through rose-colored glasses.

Having Neptune retrograde in your chart may lead to discomfort with spiritual matters. Conversely, it could prompt deep contemplation and introspection about spiritual aspects of life.

Pluto in Retrograde

Pluto experiences a retrograde phase lasting approximately 160 days each year, occurring in a continuous block. These periods hold significant importance for individuals, especially if Pluto retrograde strongly influences their chart by forming aspects with planets or angles. Pluto's impact tends to be more psychological than tangible, typically involving a process of deconstruction.

During the backward-forward-backward movement of Pluto, it resembles a shredding process, where elements in our lives are torn down, repeated, and torn down once more for good measure. While this might sound intense, it aligns with Pluto's association with rebirth. After the Plutonic storm subsides, individuals often discover a sense of shedding their old selves or experiencing a profound rebirth.

For those with Pluto retrograde in their chart, there may be a sense of holding back one's powers and a fear of being controlled.

A Note on the Sun and Moon

It's crucial to remember that the Sun and Moon do not undergo retrograde motion. Given the Earth's orbit around the Sun and the Moon's orbit around the Earth, the optical illusion described earlier is not applicable to them. Considering that the Sun rules Leo, and the Moon rules Cancer, the absence of retrograde motion for these luminaries carries significance for these zodiac signs. This lack of retrograde influence suggests a continuous forward movement in the matters associated with the houses with Cancer and Leo on their cusps, with minimal pauses.

The Three Iterations of a Retrograde

To reiterate, when a planet undergoes retrogradation, it gives the impression of moving backward, essentially retracing its previous path. Let's envision Pluto in retrograde, passing over your Sun. As the retrograde commences, Pluto starts moving backward, revisiting its recent path, which means it reverses over your Sun, bringing Pluto back onto your Sun once again. Just when you thought you had dealt with Pluto, it reappears.

This scenario applies not only when Pluto is over your Sun but also if Pluto or any other planet forms an opposition, sextile, trine, or square with your Sun or any other planet. The crux is that when a planet goes into retrograde, any recent contacts it made with your chart are reiterated and then repeated once more. Here's how it unfolds:

First, there's the forward motion, where Pluto goes over your Sun.
    Next, the retrograde cycle unfolds, providing another encounter with Pluto over your Sun.
    At the end of the retrograde, Pluto changes direction, initiating forward movement once more, resulting in yet another pass over your Sun.

These are the three phases of a retrograde. Events transpire during the forward motion, then the retrograde cycle revisits and amplifies the experience, and finally, the forward motion resumes for a concluding encounter.

This sequence can potentially occur with every retrograde,

provided it happens in the same position as, or forms an aspect to, one of your planets. There's a purpose behind this recurrence, and for those aiming to live consciously, understanding and working with this repetition is crucial. The belief is that a retrograde occurs when there's a profound lesson to be learned, and the repetition allows for a thorough understanding of the lesson over time.

In the case of challenging retrogrades involving tough planets like Mars or Saturn, making formidable aspects like squares to our planets, the goal is for each pass to bring increased awareness and mastery of handling the energies and lessons. The analogy of learning to drive illustrates the process—from being unconsciously unskilled to consciously unskilled, and finally, achieving unconscious skill.

During the first retrograde pass, you might be somewhat oblivious to the upcoming lesson. The retrograde phase heightens awareness. By the third pass, as forward motion resumes, you've acquired the skills to handle the issues consciously. Thus, during a three-pass retrograde, working consciously with the energies and reflecting on the lessons inherent in your chart becomes essential.

Days of Halting

As you delve deeper into the study of astrology, you'll encounter the concept of 'stations.' A station, in astronomical terms, refers to the moment when a planet appears to cease its regular movement in the sky from the Earth's perspective. During this point, the planet seems to gradually shift in the opposite direction, marking the phase known as stationary retrograde. Similarly, when the planet halts, then recommences its forward movement, it is termed stationary direct.

Consider Jupiter, which typically spends over half of each year in direct motion, meaning it moves forward. However, when Jupiter decelerates, halts, and reverses its direction or resumes forward motion, these transitional points are referred to as 'stations.' Astrologers would express this by saying, for instance, 'Jupiter is stationary and turning direct today' during the forward-turning phase.

In lieu of stating that Mercury is entering retrograde today, one can articulate it as 'Mercury is stationing retrograde today.' And when the retrograde concludes, and Mercury recommences its forward trajectory, it can be conveyed as 'Mercury is stationing direct.'

Periods of Influence

Another aspect of retrogrades worth noting is the concept of 'shadow' periods. This is linked to the idea that a planet's retrograde trajectory encompasses a broader range in the astrological chart – covering more degrees than just those between the official station days.

For instance, let's consider the Mercury retrograde cycle in

April 2017. On April 10, 2017, Mercury initiated its retrograde motion at 4 Taurus. The retrograde phase concluded on May 3, with Mercury stationing direct at 24 Aries. To determine the commencement of the shadow period, one needs to trace back to when Mercury was at 24 Aries, moving forward, before the retrograde began. This occurred on March 27, 2017. Hence, the shadow period commenced on March 27 and continued until Mercury returned to 4 Taurus, where the retrograde concluded – in this instance, until May 20. Therefore, the shadow period spanned from March 27 to May 20.

While personally, I don't ascribe significant importance to shadow periods, as the initiation and conclusion of a retrograde carry more potency, some astrologers find value in considering these transitional phases. It remains a matter of individual interpretation and practice within the field.

4

The Moon's Nodes

Another valuable aspect to explore on your birth chart involves the Moon's nodes, which can offer profound insights into both yourself and others. While Eastern astrology places greater emphasis on the nodes compared to Western traditions, which we primarily focus on in this book, many, including myself, find them captivating and exceptionally beneficial for comprehending the fundamental aspects of a chart and making predictions. Like planets and signs, the Moon's nodes are represented as unique symbols – glyphs.

The nodes signify the points at which the Moon intersects the ecliptic, the apparent path of the Sun as observed from Earth. The North Node marks the Moon's northward crossing of the ecliptic, while the South Node signifies its southward crossing. These two points consistently oppose each other and are typically in retrograde motion.

The South Node reveals actions and experiences from a person's past life, showcasing innate abilities and aspects of life that feel effortless or familiar. For instance, if someone has the South Node in the 7th house, relationships come naturally to them. On the opposite side of the chart lies the North Node, indicating what an individual needs to pursue and where they should direct their life to discover satisfaction, fulfillment, and happiness. Some refer to this node as indicative of life purpose. Another interpretation suggests North Node represents fame, while the South Node represents infamy.

Engaging with the Moon's Nodes

Delving into the dynamics of the nodes on our chart can be a daunting task. The underlying concept is centered around self-improvement, urging us to distance ourselves from the characteristics associated with the South Node house and progress towards the attributes of the North Node house. This journey involves a thorough examination of our behavioral patterns. Let's illustrate this with an example:

Consider an individual whose birth chart places the South Node in the 7th house, linked to love and relationships, and the North Node in the 1st house, associated with the self. According to the interpretations provided earlier, the South Node represents the comfort zone – in this scenario, a preference for relationships given the 7th house's focus. On the contrary, the North Node points to the path of growth, requiring the person to establish their independence since the 1st house pertains to the Self.

Does this imply that the individual should remain single throughout their lifetime? Not necessarily. However, it does suggest a need to cultivate independence rather than relying on codependency. Despite the allure of losing oneself in the ease of relationships (South Node, 7th house), genuine happiness and fulfillment lie in pursuing individual endeavors (North Node, 1st house).

Decoding the Significance of the Moon's Nodes

Direct your attention to the house placement of the Moon's nodes on your chart to unravel their implications for you. The following interpretations are extracted from my book Moonology (Hay House), which I recommend if you're inclined to delve deeper into understanding how the Moon and its phases influence your life.

1. North Node in the 1st house/South Node in the 7th house:
   - While fixating on relationships, discovering independence will lead to genuine happiness.

2. North Node in the 2nd house/South Node in the 8th house:
   - Despite the allure of profound and taboo subjects, focusing on financial stability brings greater joy.

3. North Node in the 3rd house/South Node in the 9th house:
   Though indulging in self-expression may seem enticing, genuine happiness arises through meaningful communication with others.

4. North Node in the 4th house/South Node in the 10th house:
   - While career aspirations may be captivating, true fulfillment lies in nurturing home and family.

5. North Node in the 5th house/South Node in the 11th house:
   - Despite the allure of friendships and freedom, authentic happiness emerges from creative self-expression.

6. North Node in the 6th house/South Node in the 12th house:
   - Escaping from life's demands may be a tempting daydream, but true fulfillment comes from facing responsibilities head-on.

7. North Node in the 7th house/South Node in the 1st house:
   - Relationships offer significant growth opportunities, even if they push your buttons.

8. North Node in the 8th house/South Node in the 2nd house:
   - Despite financial concerns, a dose of passionate intimacy is what you truly need now.

9. North Node in the 9th house/South Node in the 3rd house:
   - Opting for genuine truth over light-hearted chatter brings liberation.

10. North Node in the 10th house/South Node in the 4th house:
    - While "family first" is commendable, current cosmic influences encourage immersing yourself in your career for fulfillment.

11. North Node in the 11th house/South Node in the 5th house:
    - That person you desire romantically may be better suited

as a friend.

12. North Node in the 12th house/South Node in the 6th house:
   - Prioritizing inner peace over meticulous life organization is what truly matters.

www.ingramcontent.com/pod-product-compliance
Lightning Source LLC
LaVergne TN
LVHW020443080526
838202LV00055B/5323